Redeemed And Restored

Covenant Promises Found in Isaiah 54

A. L. Taylor

BookLeaf Publishing

India | USA | UK

Made with ❤ on the BookLeaf Publishing Platform
www.bookleafpub.in
www.bookleafpub.com

Dedication

To my Redeemer, Creator of the Universe, whose faithfulness never wavers and whose promises are always true. May these reflections bring honor to Your Word. May it bring hope to the hopeless. May it bring light to the darkness.

Thank You for never giving up on me. May I continue to grow in your truth.

And to those who said, this book would never come to pass —surprise! He makes all things possible.

Preface

This collection of poems was born from my travels through Isaiah 54—a chapter in the Bible that speaks of restoration, expansion, and unwavering divine love. It is a personal testimony to the faithfulness of the One who redeems and restores, even when the world sees only brokenness. Isaiah 54 has been the foundation of my faith, the compass I've always come back to in every season of my journey. It has guided me through the highs and lows, grounding me in the promises of Yah.

Each poem is a reflection of a season in my journey: moments of barrenness that were transformed into abundance, ashes that were turned into beauty, and promises that were fulfilled against all odds. Writing these verses was not just an exercise in creativity; it was an act of faith, a process of healing, and a declaration of trust in the One who never gives up on me and will continue His work in me until it is complete.

My hope is that these words will resonate with you, reminding you of the steadfast love of our Creator and the hope that springs eternal through His promises.

Acknowledgements

First and foremost, I give thanks to Yah, my Redeemer, Creator, and Sustainer. Without His unwavering faithfulness, this collection would not exist. His love, grace, and strength have been the foundation of my journey, and through every season, He has been my guiding light.

To my mom, who has been the tough love I never knew I needed, your strength and no-nonsense approach have pushed me to reach beyond what I thought was possible. Your love has never wavered, even during the times we didn't see eye to eye. I am forever grateful for the lessons you've given me.

To my daughter, who has been my divine purpose, your light has been a constant reminder of God's grace and the reason I strive to keep moving forward. Keep adjusting your crown and remember to whom you belong.

To my sons, who I may not have born but whom I have had the privilege of raising—thank you for teaching me so much about God's love. Through both struggle and strength, you have shaped my understanding of grace, patience, and unconditional love. I am deeply grateful for the lessons you have imparted, and for the ways you've each contributed to the growth of my heart.

To Calvin, for guiding me toward Yah and pointing me in the right direction — the wisdom you imparted continues to shape my faith journey.

And finally, to the rest of my family and friends that have supported me, whether near or far, your encouragement and prayers have been a blessing beyond measure.

The Barren Woman Sings

(Inspired by Isaiah 54:1)

Sing, O barren one, lift your voice,
Though desolation dulled your choice.
For many shall be your children still,
Birthed not by flesh, but by God's will.
Cry out, you who knew no womb's delight,
For your tent will stretch to fill the night.
North and south will hear your song,
East and west will come along.
Fear not, for shame will be erased,
Your Maker's hand will lift your face.
The past is past, the promise new—
A family forged from love so true.
So, sing aloud, though tears once burned;
The barren land has now returned.
A harvest blooms where none had sown,
For you are called by God's own throne.

A Tent Without Borders

(Inspired by Isaiah 54:2–3)

Stretch the cords, expand your space,
Lengthen stakes to claim your place.
Your tent will house the nations wide,
A promise kept, your faiths abide.

The cities ruined, long left bare,
Will brim with life beyond compare.
No walls can hold what He will do,
No gates contain His love for you.

Lift your hammer, mend the stake,
Lay foundations that won't break.
For barren days are far behind,
And joy replaces the weary mind.

No Fear of the Night

(Inspired by Isaiah 54:4)

Do not fear the night.
The shadows no longer have power over your name.
Once they gripped you with their cold embrace,
but now, you stand free, unshaken.
The storm may rage,
winds may howl,
but your feet are firm,
your heart anchored in peace.
Fear that once whispered in your ear,
has been cast out.
You no longer walk in shame,
for righteousness has clothed you.
He has wiped away the years.
Your dawn has broken,
shadows flee—
A covenant love stands eternally.

Your Husband, Your Redeemer

(Inspired by Isaiah 54:5-6)

You are no longer forsaken,
Abandoned to sorrow's embrace.
Your Maker is your Husband,
He has called you by name.
The Lord of Hosts has chosen you,
Redeemer of all, the Holy One.
The God of Israel calls you His own,
His love a light that shines like the sun.
Once, your days were empty,
Now, they overflow with grace.
Where tears once fell in silence,
Now joy fills every space.
His covenant whispers dispel your fears,
No longer forsaken,
No longer alone,
You are redeemed,
And you are His own.

Like Waters Gone

(Inspired by Isaiah 54:6-9)

For a moment, He turned His face
But everlasting is His embrace.
Like Noah's flood, His wrath has ceased,
And now His mercy is your peace.

A woman forsaken, grieving, alone,
Called back to the arms of the Throne.
"I swore the waters would never return,
So too, My kindness will steadfastly burn."

The hills may shake, the earth may fall,
But steadfast love outlasts it all.
He binds you close with covenant care,
No wrath remains, just grace laid bare.

Stones of Sapphire

(Inspired by Isaiah 54: 11-12)

Afflicted one, tossed by the waves,
I lay your foundation where glory saves.
Stones of sapphire, walls of flame,
Each gate adorned with My holy name.

Your towers rise, aglow with peace,
Every stone a masterpiece.
A city rebuilt from desolation,
A sign of eternal consecration.

No storm can shake what I have laid,
No hand can undo the plans I've made.
In sapphire light, your strength will show,
For you are Mine - this you will know.

Children of Peace

(Inspired by Isaiah 54:13)

All my children taught by Me,
Shall walk in truth and harmony.
Their peace will flow like streams of gold,
A promise kept, a future bold.
No shadows will fall where they will tread,
No fear will haunt where I have led.
The wisdom sown, the lessons learned,
Will light the path for which they yearned.
My household, blessed beyond compare,
Each child a jewel, divinely rare.
Their peace shall stand as testament,
My covenant gift
magnificent.

Righteousness Stands

(Inspired by Isaiah 54:14)

Established in righteousness, firm you stand,
No terror shall rise by My command.

Oppression flees, and fear takes flight,
For justice dawns with morning's light.

No weapon formed will strike you down,
No schemes of darkness steal your crown.

With walls of peace and truth your shield,
The fruit of faith will never yield.

In righteousness, you take your place,
A nation built on mercy's grace.

No trembling heart, no faltering hand,
You are secure where I command.

The morning sun will rise with power,
And peace will reign in every hour.

The winds of change will bow before,
The strength of those who trust and soar.

In My embrace, you stand unshaken,
For every promise has been taken.

No enemy will stand before,
The One who calls, the One who's more.

Through every trial, through every storm,
In righteousness, you will be reborn.

The Gathering

(Inspired by Isaiah 54:7-8)

For a moment, He stepped away,
The heavens dimmed, and silence fell.
Yet His love, deeper than the oceans,
Bore you home on waves of mercy.
He called you back -
Not as servant,
Not as stranger,
But as His own.
"In overflowing wrath,
I hid Myself for but a blink.
Now, in endless lovingkindness,
I embrace you."
Hear it: the voice of eternity.
Feel it: the arms of redemption.
You are gathered,
You are His.

The Covenant's Thread

(Inspired by Isaiah 54:9–10)

The mountains quake; the rivers roar.
Empires fall and are no more.
Yet My promise, a golden thread,
Woven through time, holds where I've led.
To Noah, I vowed the floods would cease,
A covenant carved in eternal peace.
Now to you, beloved and dear,
I swear again: no wrath, no fear.
Though hills erode and oceans fade,
My steadfast kindness will not evade.
My love stands firm, unshaken, whole,
A tether unbroken, binding your soul.

A City Reborn

(Inspired by Isaiah 54:11–12)

O storm-tossed city, weary walls,
Where chaos reigns and silence calls—

Look! Your foundations rise anew,
Every stone a promise, true.

Ruby gates and sparkling towers,
Streets that sing of heavenly hours.

Once forgotten, now restored,
A dwelling fit for your Lord.

No more ashes, no more dust,
No decay, no breach, no rust.

Only beauty, radiant, bright,
A city reborn in eternal light.

He who formed you, now remakes,
The sorrow of your past He breaks.

The Lord of Hosts will stand by you,
His faithfulness will see you through.

No weapon formed against you thrives,
No tongue that rises against you survives.

For your Redeemer is strong and near,
In His covenant, you'll have no fear.

Your gates are peace, your walls are grace,
His righteousness will light your face.

He will build you, He will restore,
A city of promise forevermore.

Weaponless Fear

(Inspired by Isaiah 54:15–17)

They'll gather, yes,
but not by My hand.
Their schemes will crumble,
their plots like sand.
See the smith at the forge,
hammering steel into flame.
Yet every weapon he fashions
will shatter against your name.
No whisper, no word,
no insult can stand.
Every tongue that accuses
will fall by My hand.
The storms may rise,
the winds may howl,
But you are hidden in My peace,
where none can reach or prowl.
Though the earth may shake,
and the heavens burn,

If you dwell in My shadow,
there, no harm can return.
I am your refuge,
your place of rest,
The shelter of your soul,
where you are blessed.
Their fury is fleeting,
their might is undone,
For I hold the light,
where dark shadows are none.
This is your heritage;
this is your right:
No weapon formed against you
will ever take flight.
You are woven in My will,
a tapestry unbroken,
And in My hand,
you are forever chosen.

The Maker's Hands

(Inspired by Isaiah 54:5)

He who spread the heavens,
Who painted galaxies with His word,
Has bound Himself to you.
Maker of mountains,
Shaper of seas,
He calls you bride.
You are not forgotten,
Not a flicker in the void.
You are the work of His hands,
Beloved, adorned, His treasure.
What can separate you?
Not the cosmos.
Not time.
Not even yourself.
Your Maker is your Redeemer,
The Holy One of Israel.

The Eternal Yes

(Inspired by Isaiah 54:10)

The mountains groan beneath the sky,
Ridges crumble, rivers run dry.
Kingdoms rise, and kingdoms fall—
Still, His mercy outlasts it all.
The heavens speak a single truth,
From ancient days to eternal youth:
"I will not leave; My love won't fade.
This covenant of peace I've made."
So fear no quake, no flood, no flame,
His "Yes" remains, unchanging, the same.
While time unwinds and worlds reset,
His promise stands—unbroken yet.

A Bride Adorned

(Inspired by Isaiah 54:5-6)

Come forth, O widow,
O bride once scorned.
Your veil is lifted,
Your shame outworn.
The One who formed the heavens vast,
Who holds tomorrow, today, and past,
Now calls you home, His chosen bride,
No longer wandering, cast aside.
"I am your Husband," declares the King,
"My love forever, My heart I bring."
No shadow lingers, no tear remains,
Only joy within My holy domains.
Your dress is woven with threads of gold,
Your story redeemed, your worth untold.
Lift your head and behold the skies—
You are His jewel, His sacred prize.

Fear's Exile

(Inspired by Isaiah 54:4 and 14)

Fear packs its bags,
For you've evicted it.
Shame leaves no forwarding address.
The ruins are rebuilt,
Each stone kissed with peace.
Oppression's echo fades into silence.
You walk unshaken,
Feet firm in righteousness.
No more trembling.
No more running.
Instead, laughter spills into the streets,
And joy flings open the windows.
This is your home now—
Solid, safe, eternal.

The Great Exchange

(Inspired by Isaiah 54:7-8)

He turned away,
just for a moment,
as the storms raged around.

But now He calls,
with a voice like sunrise:
"Come back to Me, My beloved."

Wrath is buried in the past,
flooded by mercy's tide.
Anger dissolved,
kindness remains.

Abandonment traded
for an embrace,
silence
for everlasting love.

A Banner Over Your Children

(Inspired by Isaiah 54:13)

Over your children, a banner flies,
In letters written across the skies:
"Peace is their portion, grace their light,
Guided forever by My sight."
Not carved in stone, but in the heart,
A love that never will depart.
Though they may wander, stray, and roam,
My love will always bring them home.
Like mighty oaks, their roots entwine,
In fields of grace, they will always shine.
Watched by the Shepherd, who guards with care,
His constant presence, always there.
When they are lost, He will pursue,
With every step, He'll carry through.
And you, their mother, will stand and see,
The fruit of His promise—eternity.

Foundations of Flame

(Inspired by Isaiah 54:11-12)

Rubies glint where ashes fell
Topaz gleams where shadows dwelled

A foundation of flame, a city aglow,
Built by a Builder whose craft you now know

Every gate a jewel, every wall a light,
Dispelling the darkness, defeating the night.

You are a city, redeemed, restored,
A dwelling place for your covenant Lord.

No winds will topple what He has designed,
No waters will erode the work of His mind.

Shine, O city, a beacon of grace -
The holy reflection of your Maker's face

The Promise of Peace

(Inspired by Isaiah 54:13-17)

In the quiet, peace will fall,
Like morning light that warms us all.

Not the absence of the storm,
But the calm that keeps the soul reborn.

The world may rage, the nations roar,
But peace will guard you evermore.

Not just a moment, not just a day,
But a peace that leads you all the way.

Though shadows loom, though winds may bend,
I am your peace, I'll never end.

Like rivers flowing soft and deep,
My promises are yours to keep.

In every trial, in every fear,
Know that My peace is drawing near.

The mountains may fall, the earth may quake,
But in My peace, you will never break.

So rest, My child, in love's embrace,
For I will fill your heart with grace.

You are My own, and I will keep
The promises of peace, so sweet.

Everlasting Embrace

(Inspired by the entirety of Isaiah 54)

Sing, O barren, your silence is broken!
The desert blooms where no seed was sown.
Expand your tents; stretch wide your borders,
For His children will gather and call it home.

Fear not the shadows of days gone by,
Nor the shame that once stained your name.
For He who called the stars into being
Will cover your wounds with eternal flame.

In a moment, He hid His face,
Yet now His kindness floods the skies.
Mountains may crumble, hills may falter,
But His covenant stands, His love never dies.

O afflicted city, storm-tossed and battered,
Behold your walls of sapphire stone.
No weapon forged shall breach your fortress,
No voice of condemnation shall make you alone.

Peace will teach your children well,
Justice will anchor your righteous stand.
You are His bride, adorned in glory,
Held forever in His sovereign hand.

www.ingramcontent.com/pod-product-compliance
Lightning Source LLC
Chambersburg PA
CBHW070724160726
48003CB00006BA/2363